KINGFISHER
Larousse Kingfisher Chambers Inc.
95 Madison Avenue
New York, New York 10016

First American edition 1994
2 4 6 8 10 9 7 5 3 1

LIBRARY OF CONGRESS CATALOGING-IN-PUBLICATION DATA
Rice, Melanie.
Our world / by Melanie Rice.—1st American ed.
p.   cm.—(Little library)
Includes index.
1. Geography—Juvenile literature.   [1. Geography.]   I. Title.
II. Series: Little library (New York. N.Y.)
0133.R54   1994
910—dc20   93-51028 CIP AC

Series editor: Sue Nicholson
Editors: Brigid Avison, Hazel Poole
Cover design: Terry Woodley
Design: Ben White Associates
Cover Illustration: Lesley Smith
Illustrations on pp 15 & 27 by Maggie Brand
(Maggie Mundy Agency)
and title page & pp 16, 21 & 26–27 by Stephen Holmes
(Eunice McMullen)

ISBN 1-85697-506-1

Printed in Great Britain

Our World

Chris and Melanie Rice
Illustrated by Lesley Smith

Kingfisher

NEW YORK

Contents

Our amazing world

Our world is called the Earth. It's one of nine planets whirling around a star we call the Sun. The Earth is the only planet we know of with living things. Oceans, deserts, mountains, and forests are homes for all sorts of amazing plants, animals, and people!

Life in cold lands is very different . . .

. . . from life in hot places.

Around the world

The Earth is covered by vast stretches of water called oceans and huge blocks of land.

Arct

NORTH
AMERICA

*Pacific
Ocean*

*Atlantic
Ocean*

SOUTH
AMERICA

Most continents have a mixture of forests and farmlands, mountains and flat lands, and hot or cold lands.

On maps, this land is divided into seven big areas called continents. Except for Australia, each continent is divided up into lots of different countries. The biggest continent of all is Asia.

ean

ROPE

ASIA

Pacific
Ocean

Indian
Ocean

RICA

AUSTRALIA

ANTARCTICA

Dry places

Deserts are dry areas that have little or no rain. The driest place in the world is the Atacama Desert in South America. Until recently, it hadn't rained there for 400 years! Many deserts are hot and sandy, but not all. Some are cold, and some are covered in gravel or bare rock.

Although there isn't a lot of water, some kinds of animals still live in deserts. In hot deserts, most animals hide in the shade during the day and look for food at night, when it's cooler.

Camels can go for days without water, so people use them to carry things across the desert.

In hot, dry lands people live near waterholes called oases.

Snowy places

Some parts of the world are so freezing cold that they're always coated in snow and ice.

In snowy countries, even machines run on skis!

The coldest and snowiest places are the Antarctic continent in the far south, and the lands around the Arctic Ocean in the far north.

▽ Polar bears live in snowy lands around the Arctic Ocean. Their thick fur helps to keep them warm.

△ Penguins are only found in southern parts of the world. Many live in Antarctica.

Forest lands

Forests of tall beautiful trees cover a large part of the Earth's land. Conifer trees grow best in places with very cold winters. These trees have cones and needlelike leaves. Broad-leaved trees like warmer weather. Unlike conifers, they lose their leaves in winter.

▽ Many deer live in broad-leaved forests.

△ Wildcats live in some conifer forests.

Thick rain forests grow in places where it is always hot and wet. The rain forests are home to over half of all the kinds of animals and plants on Earth.

LEAFY PICTURES

Go on a leaf hunt, and then make a stunning leaf collage.

1 Soak the leaves in warm water until soft. Blot them dry with paper towels, then press under some heavy books for about a week.

2 Arrange leaves of different colors and shapes into a picture on a large sheet of paper.

3 Draw or paint a background, then glue down the leaves. Leave it to dry.

High mountains

Long mountain ranges run for hundreds of miles across the Earth — on the land, and even beneath the oceans.

Mountain country is usually windy. It's often cold as well, particularly during the night. In some mountain ranges, it's so cold that the ice and snow never melt.

Some of the animals that live high up on mountains have thick shaggy fur to keep them warm. Mountain goats are sure-footed, leaping from rock to rock without falling.

People living in the mountains of South America keep animals called llamas.

Water for life

We could not live on the Earth without water. We drink it, we use it for cooking and washing, and we also need it for farming. It is because water is so important to us that settlements are often found close to rivers and streams.

These villagers use the river to water their fields, wash clothes — and to splash around in!

The water for towns and cities comes from rivers and big lakes called reservoirs. It is cleaned and then pumped through pipes to homes, stores, and offices.

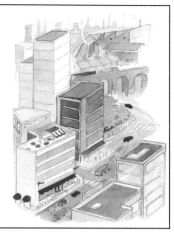

Rivers can be used as roads, too!

People of the world

There are about 190 countries in the world today, and over 5 billion people — that's enough people to fill 300 large football stadiums every day for a year! In each country people have their own customs, beliefs, and languages.

SOME NUMBERS OF THE WORLD					
English	1	2	3	4	5
Chinese	一	二	三	四	五
Bengali	১	২	৩	৪	৫
Hindi	१	२	३	४	५
Arabic	١	٢	٣	٤	٥

As many as 5,000 languages are spoken around the world.

There are many different ways of writing, as well as of speaking.

Here's how people say "hello" in some other languages.

All sorts of food

People in every country of the world have their own special foods and recipes. The things people eat mainly depend on the plants and animals that grow best in their particular country, and how much money they have to buy food.

Can you match these dishes to their country — Jamaica, China, Mexico, India, Italy, and Greece?

① Curry and rice

② Spaghetti

③ Dolmades

④ Salt-fish pie

⑤ Tacos

⑥ Noodles

People at work

One thing is the same in every country — there are jobs to be done! All over the world farmers grow food, builders make houses, and teachers help people to learn. People are busy everywhere — in towns, in the countryside, at sea, and even under the ground!

Some miners work deep underground.

Some fishermen catch fish out at sea.

People are busy at home...

...and at work...

...and having fun!

People at play

People in every country have festival days that they celebrate by dressing in their best clothes, eating special food, and giving out presents. Sometimes there are colorful street parades, too.

At Chinese New Year, parades are often led by a giant dragon!

FESTIVAL LANTERNS

Make paper lanterns for festival celebrations at home.

1 Cut wrapping paper into pieces about 4 by 6 inches and fold in half.

2 Make a row of even cuts along the folded side. Don't cut right to the edge.

3 Open out the paper and glue the sides together to make a tube.

4 Add a paper handle. Cut out a candle and tie it to the handle with thread.

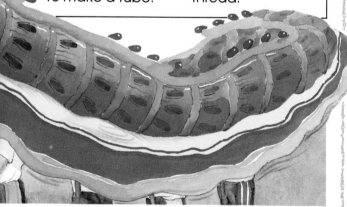

Some special words

Country   An area of land that is independent — this means it has its own border and flag, and it is run by the people who live there.

Custom   The usual way of doing something. All over the world, people have different customs about things like clothes, food, and how to behave.

Planet   A space body that moves around a star. The planets spinning around the Sun are Mercury, Venus, Earth, Mars, Jupiter, Saturn, Uranus, Neptune, and Pluto.

Index